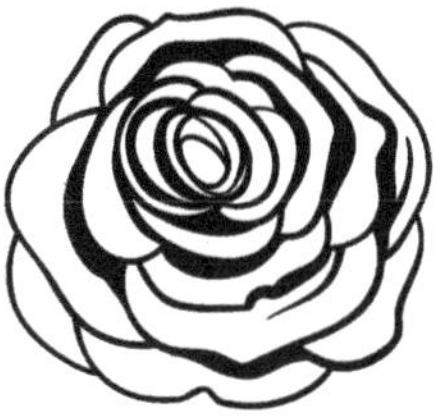

This book belongs to:

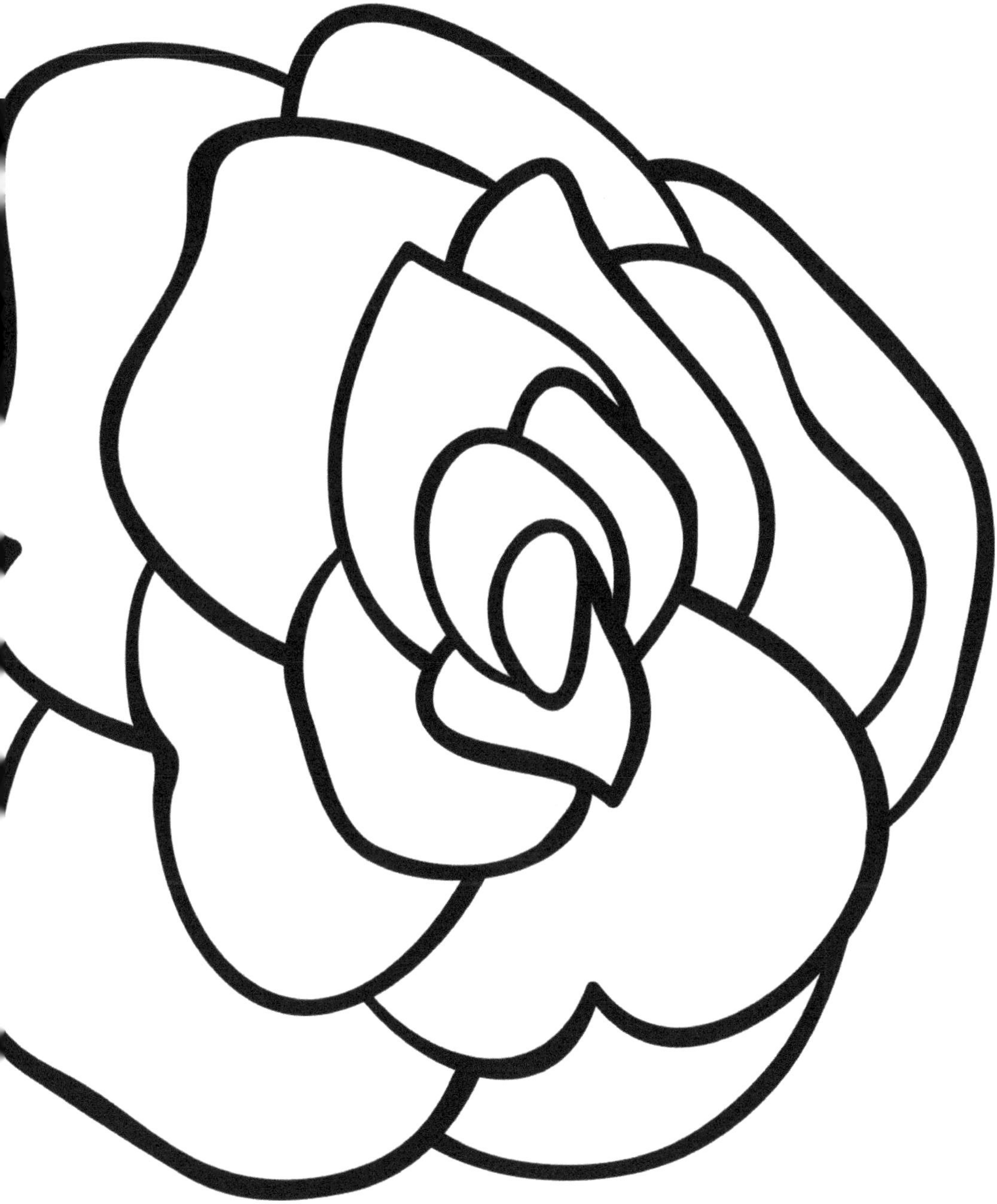

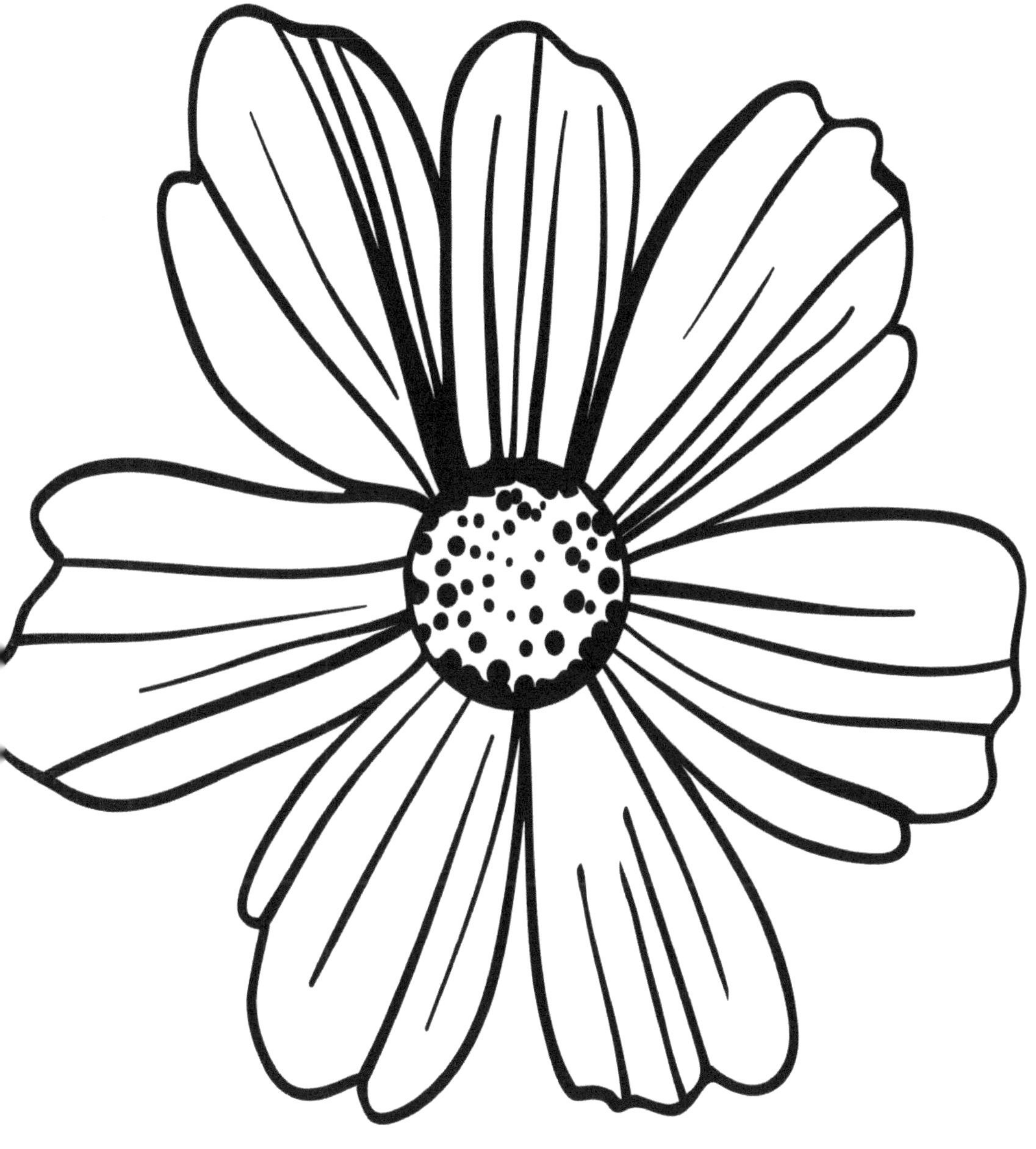

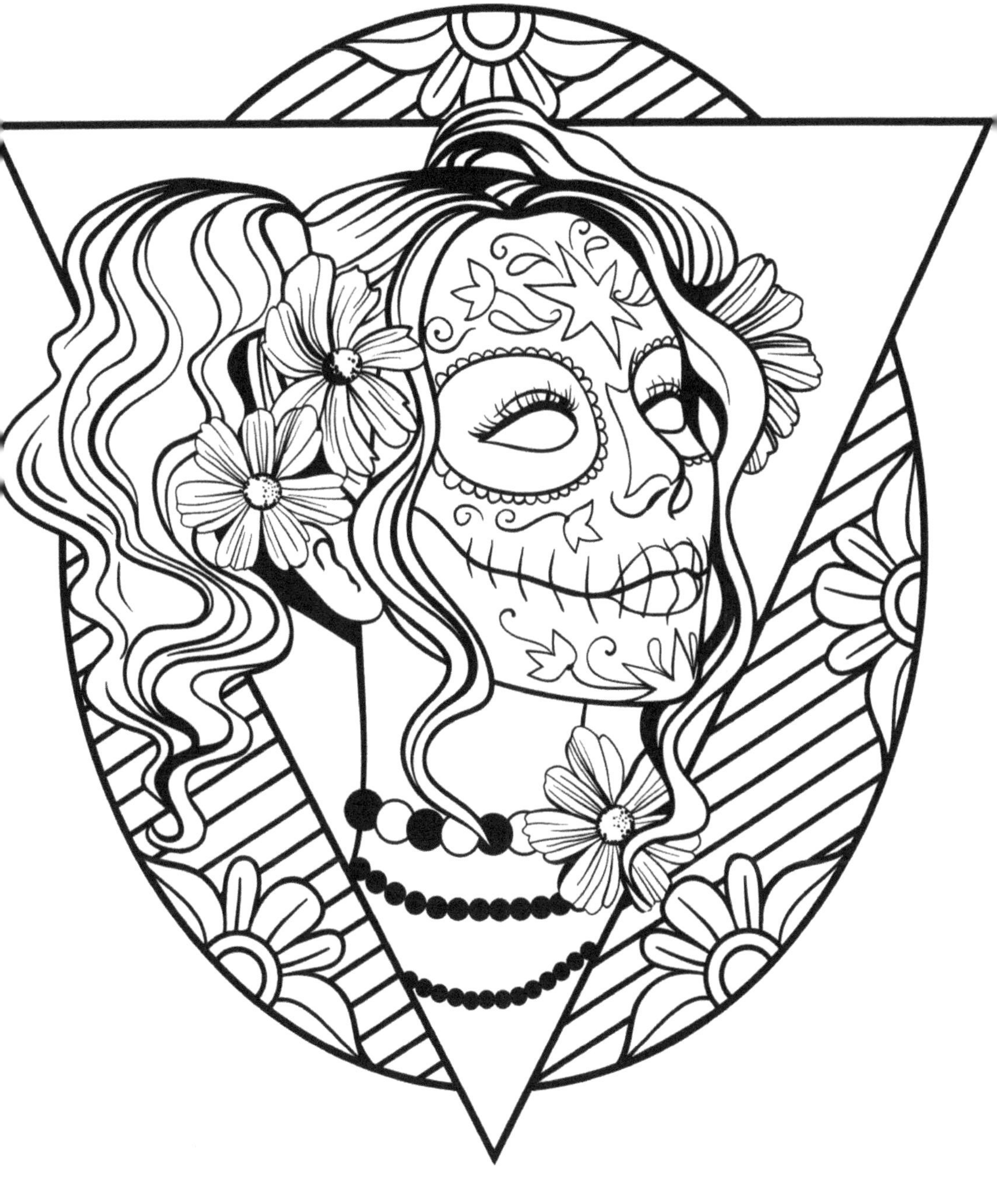

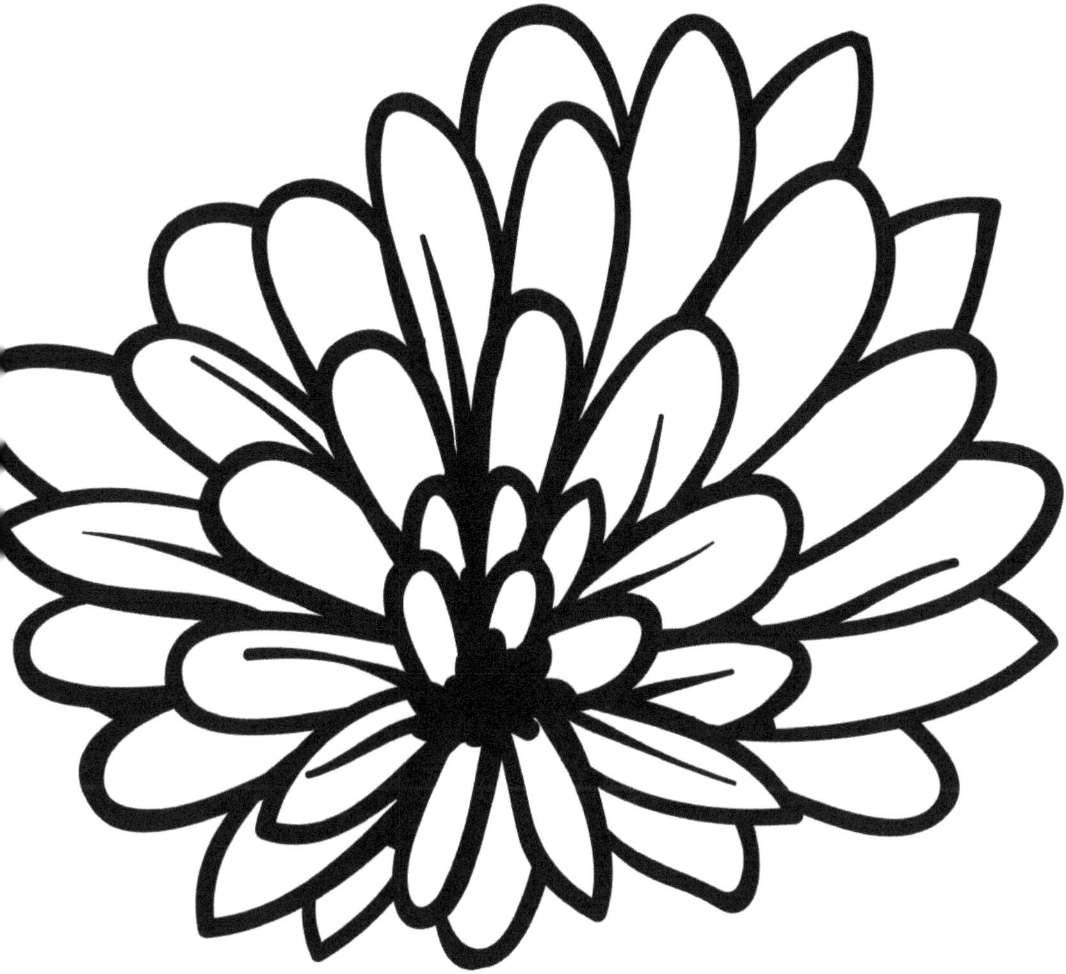

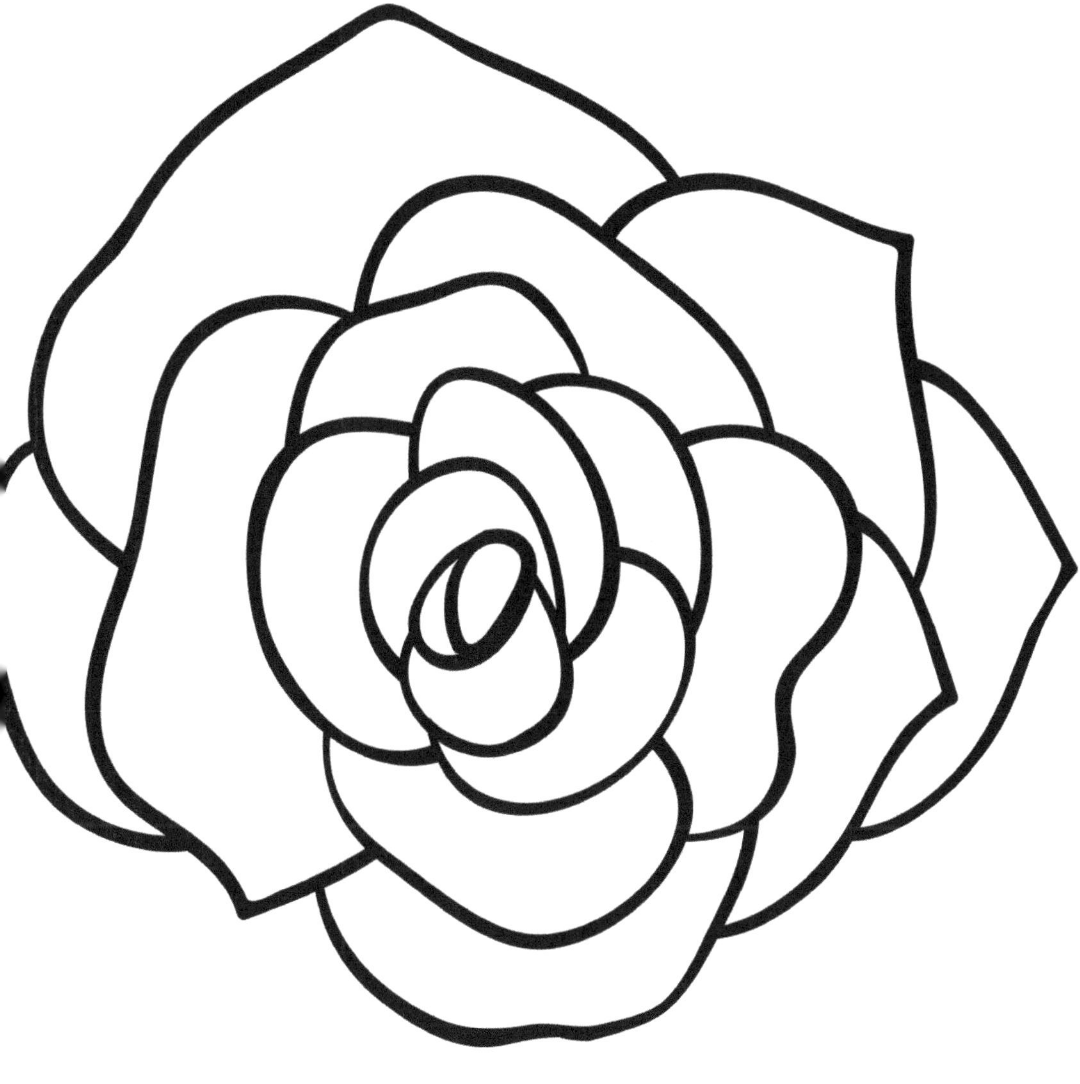

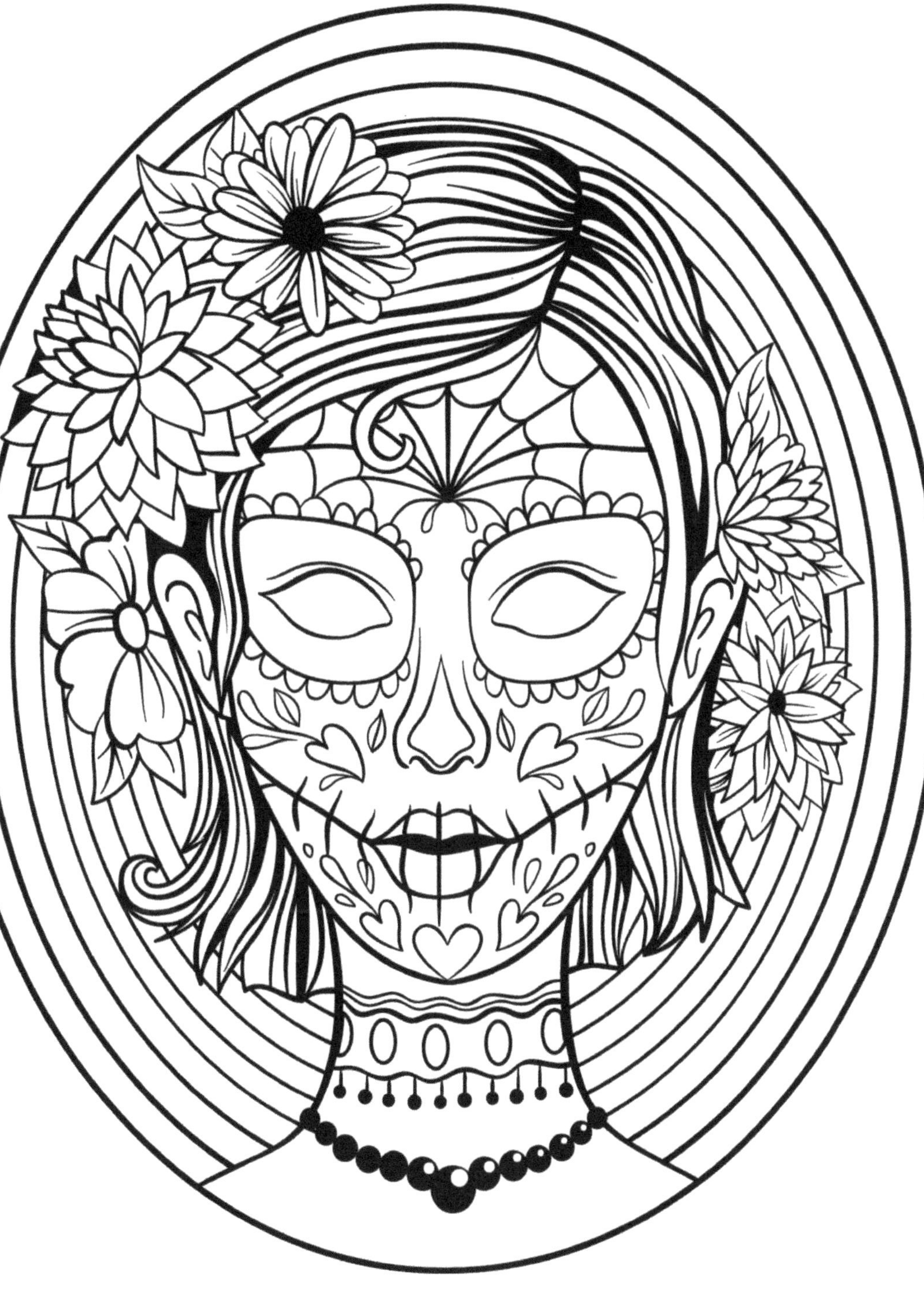

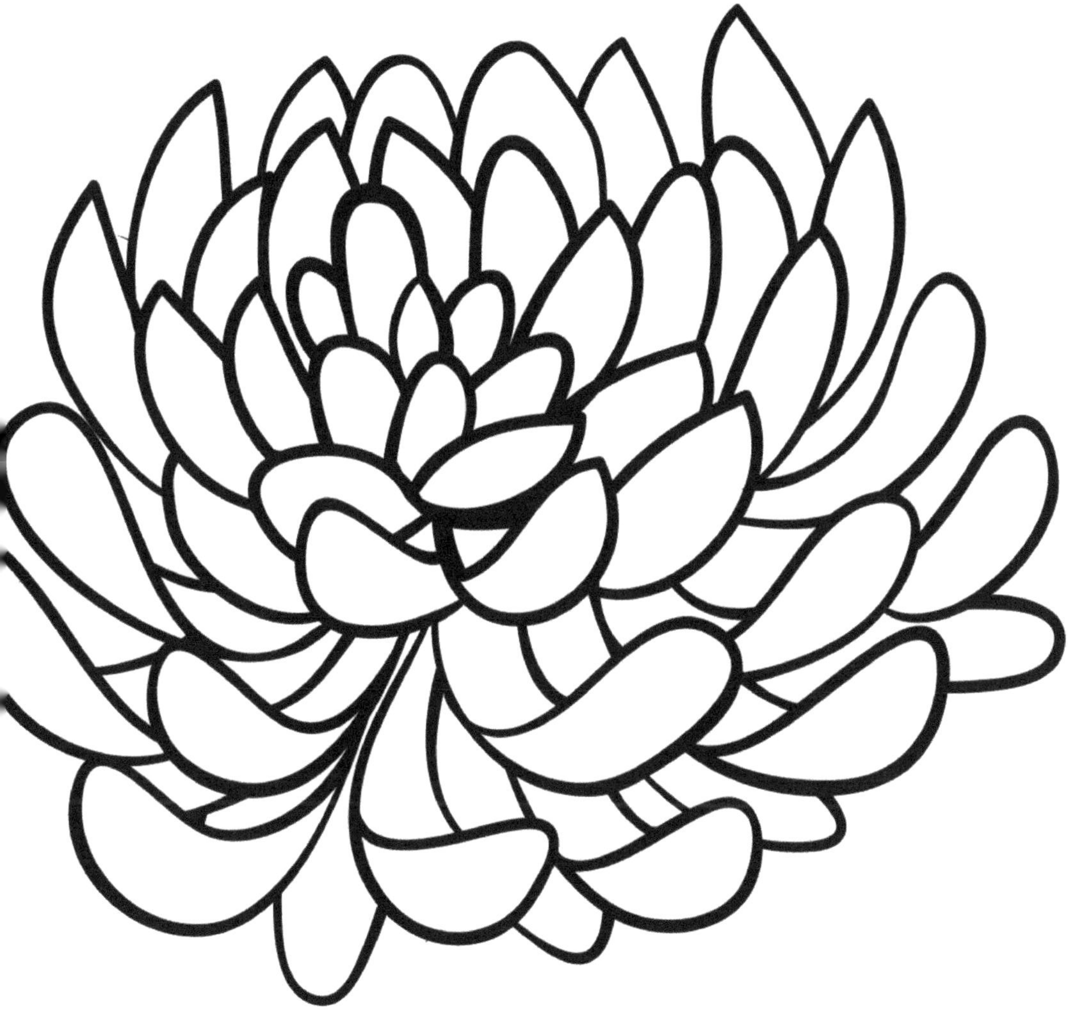

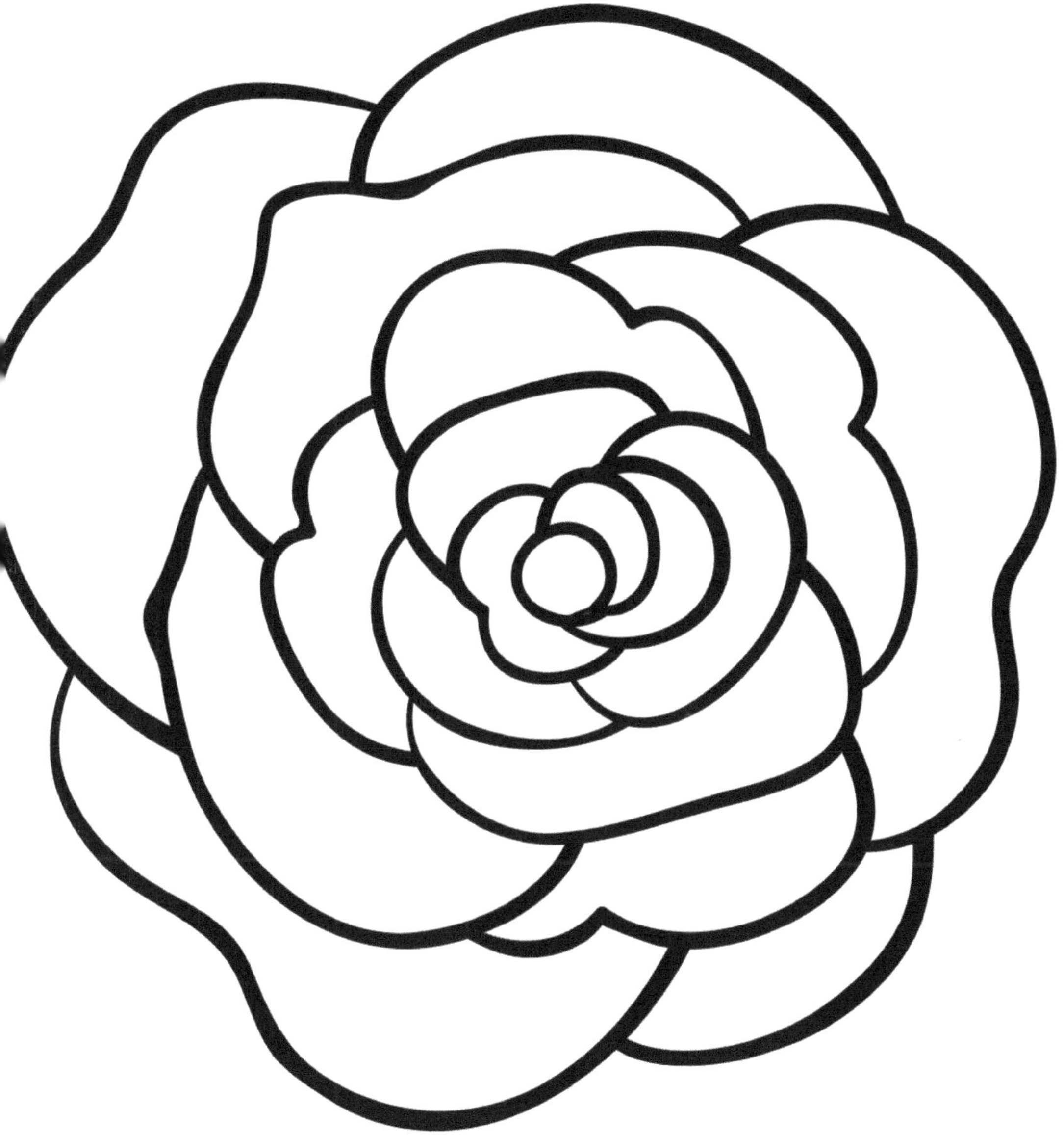

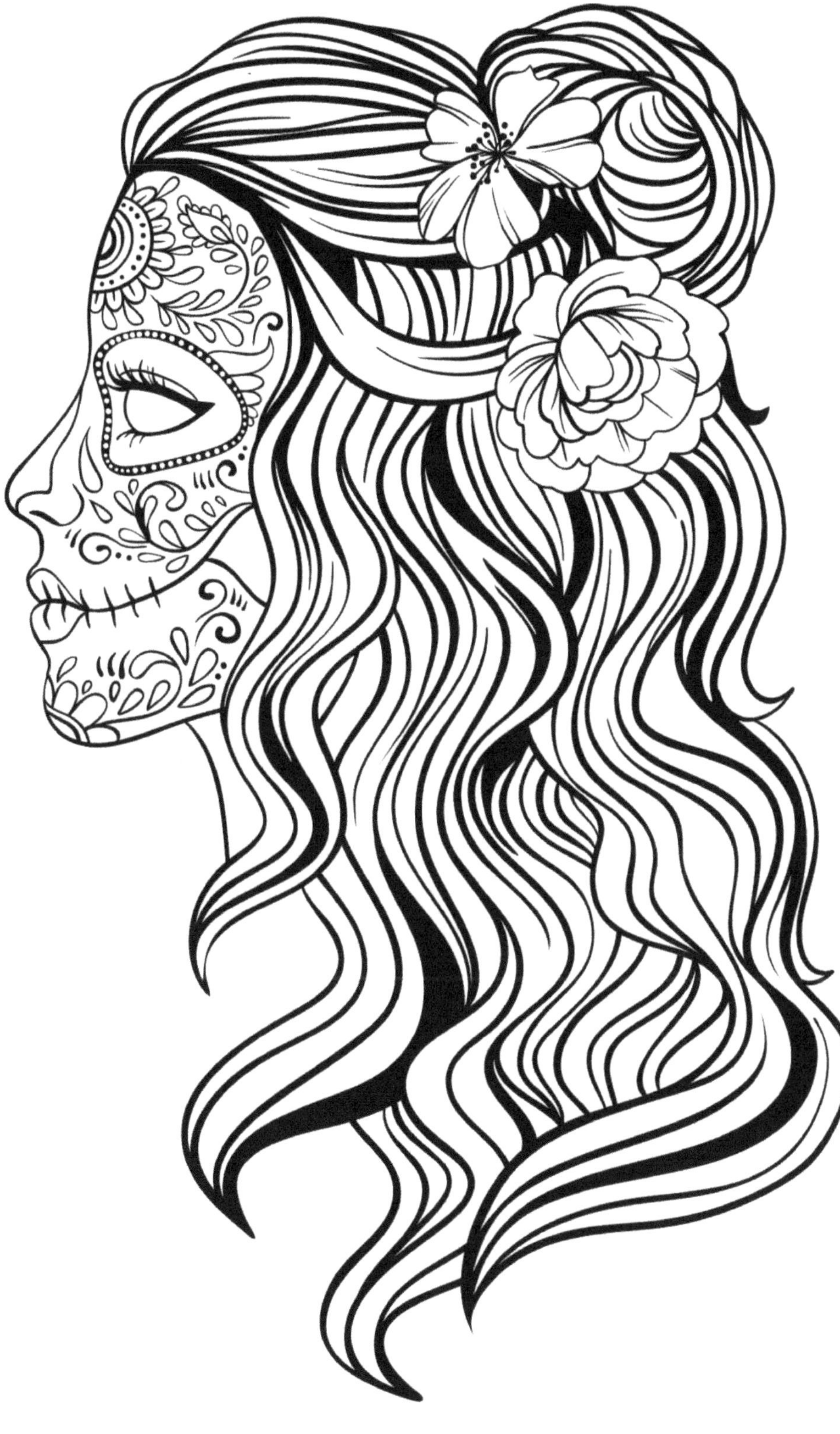

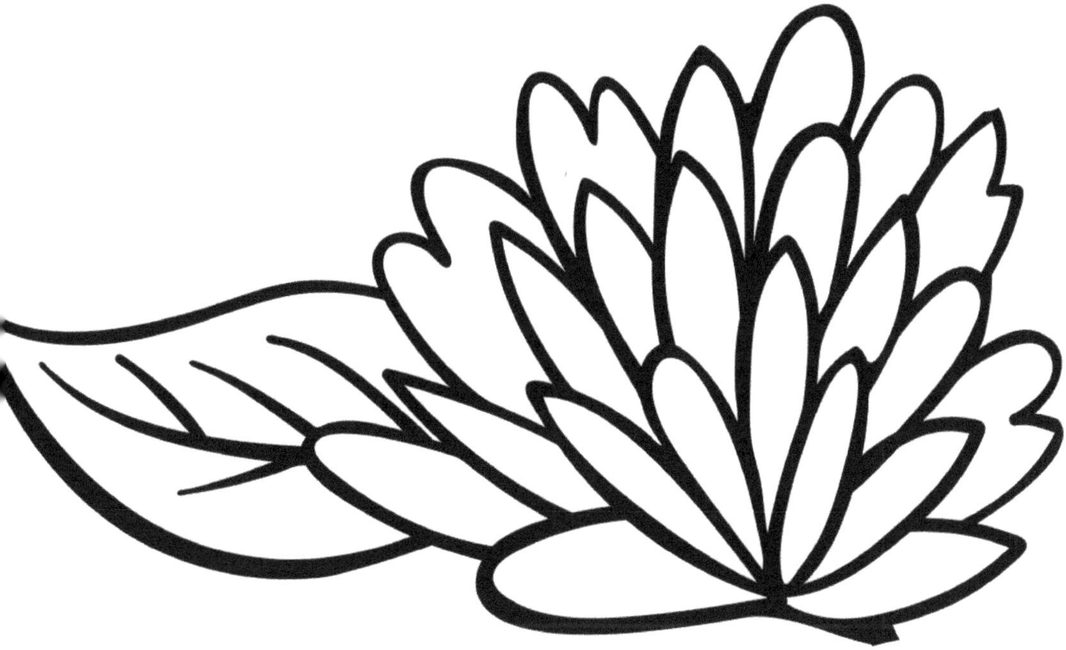

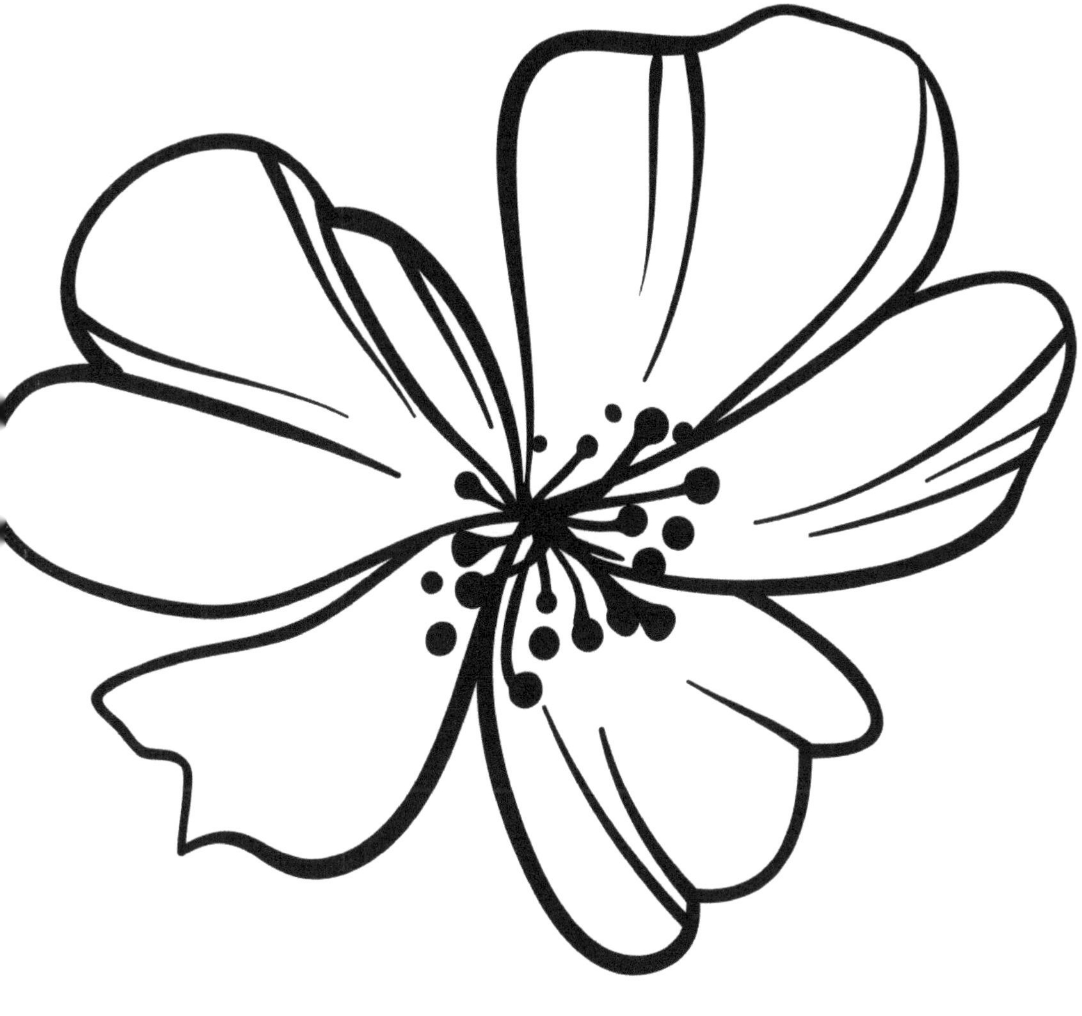

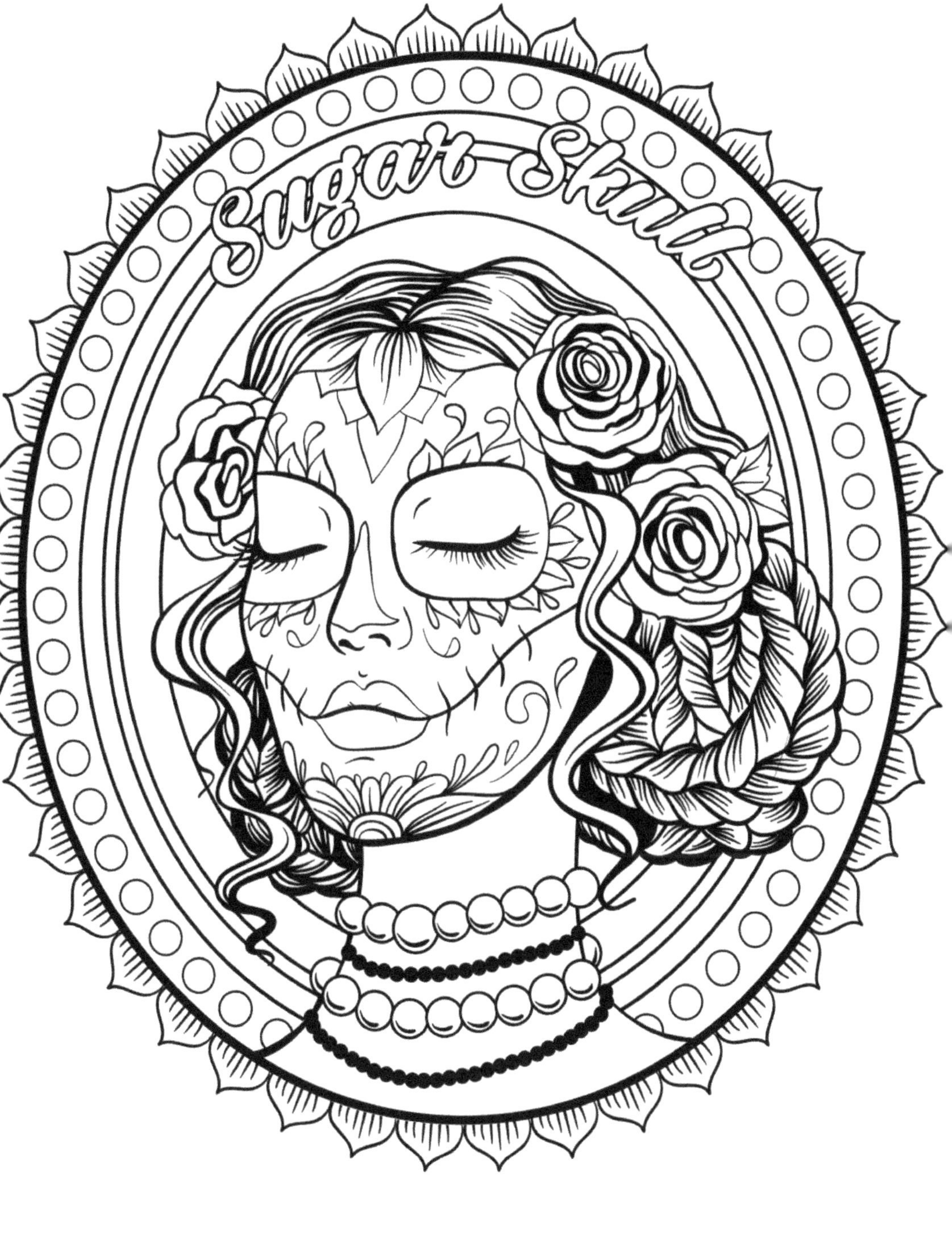
Sugar Skull

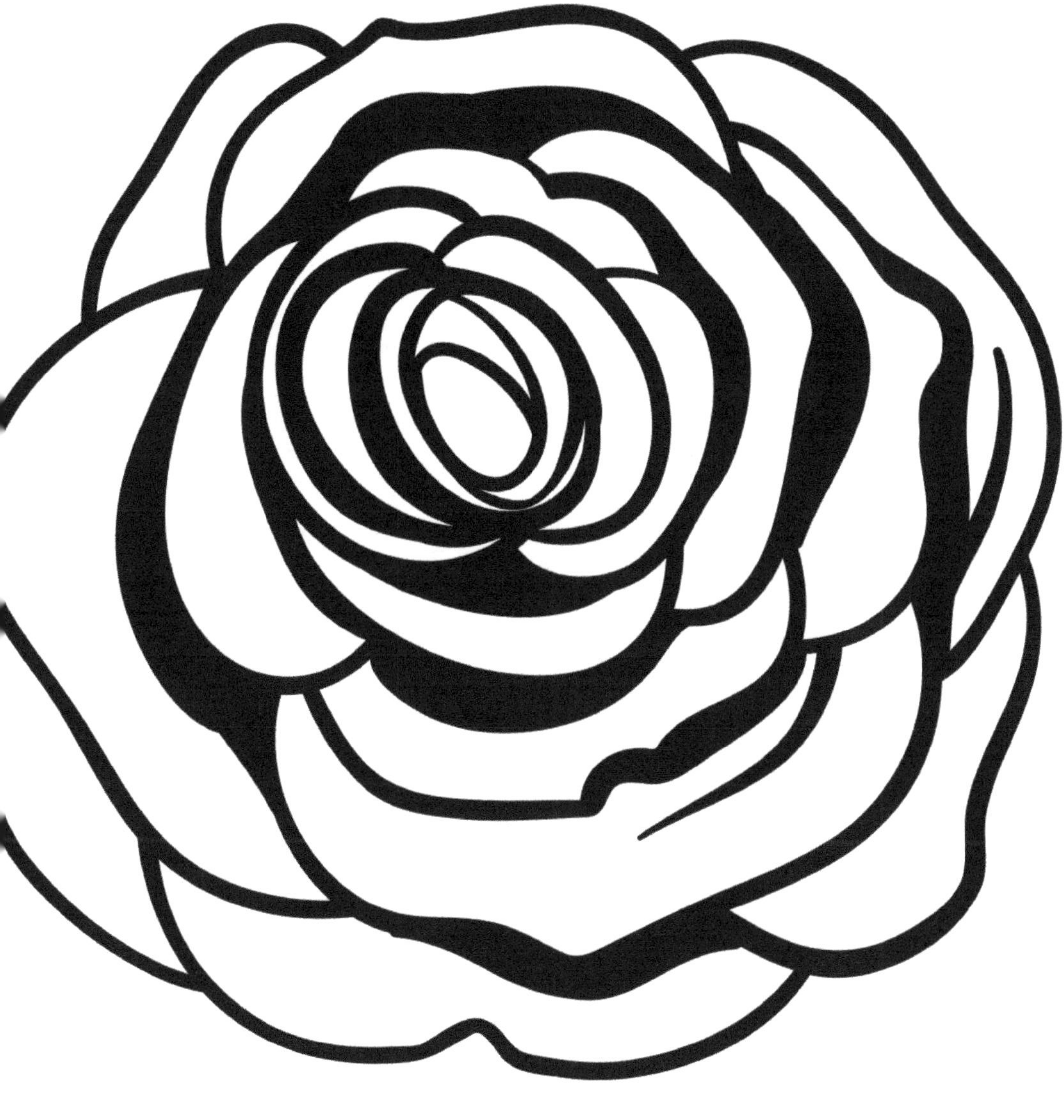

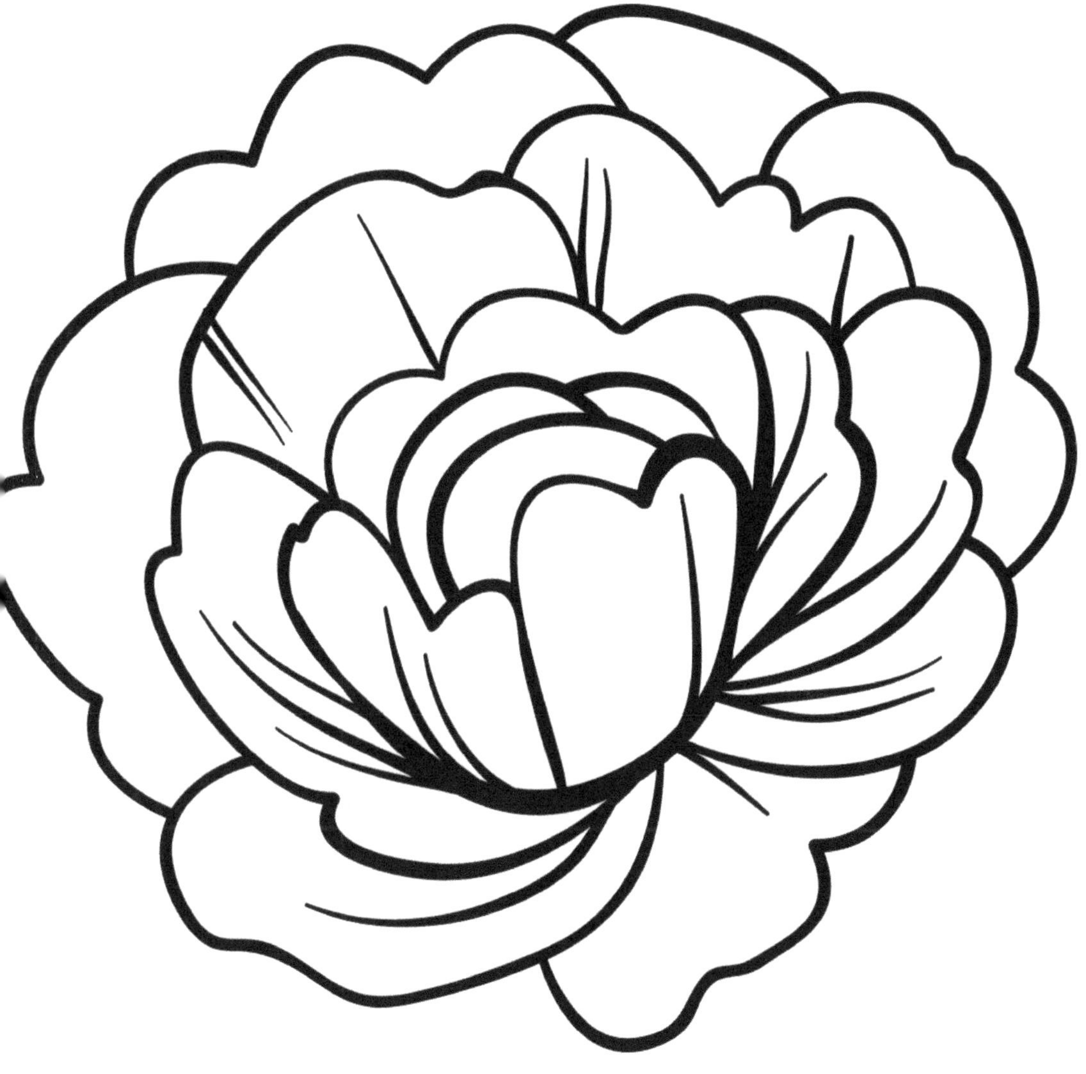

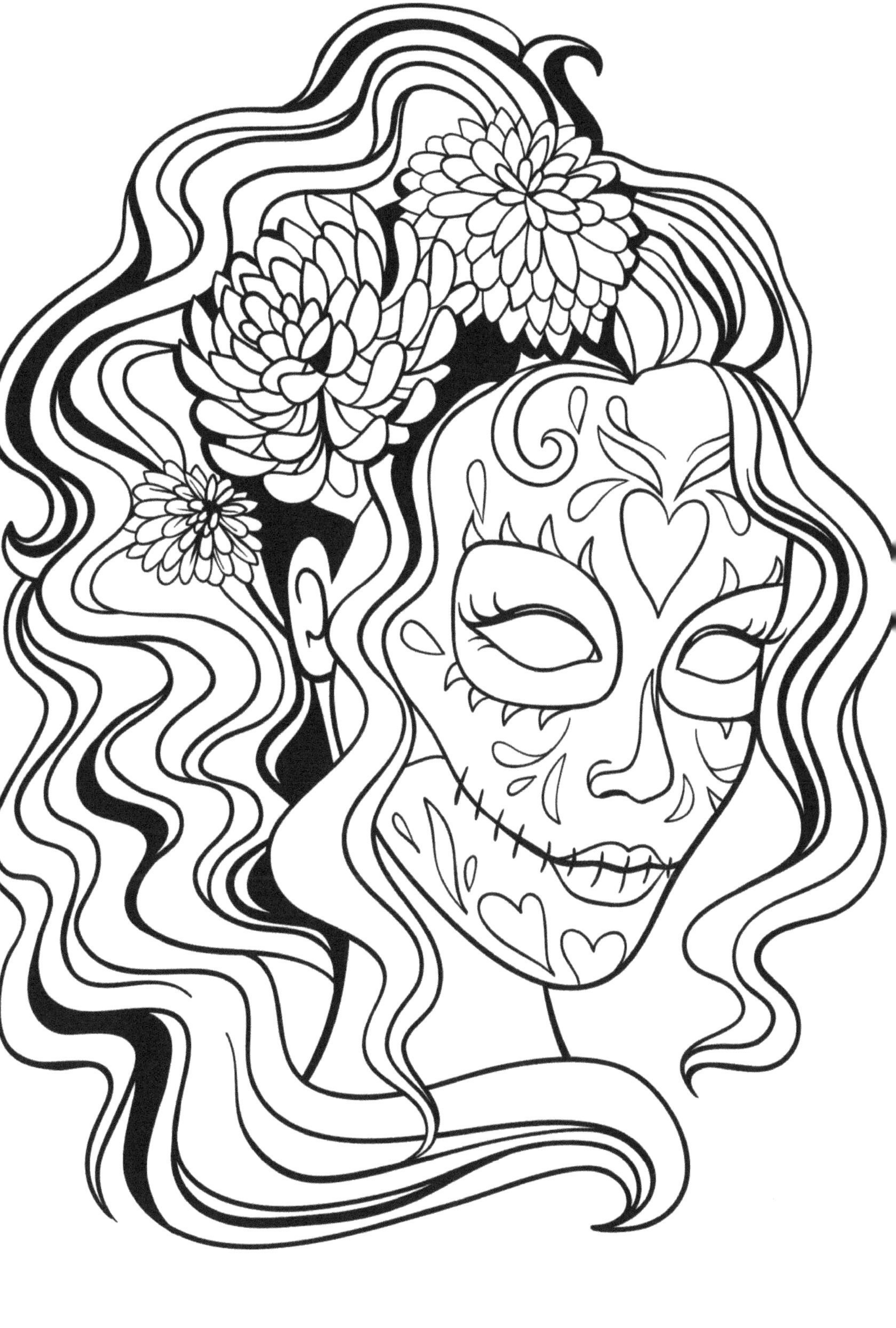

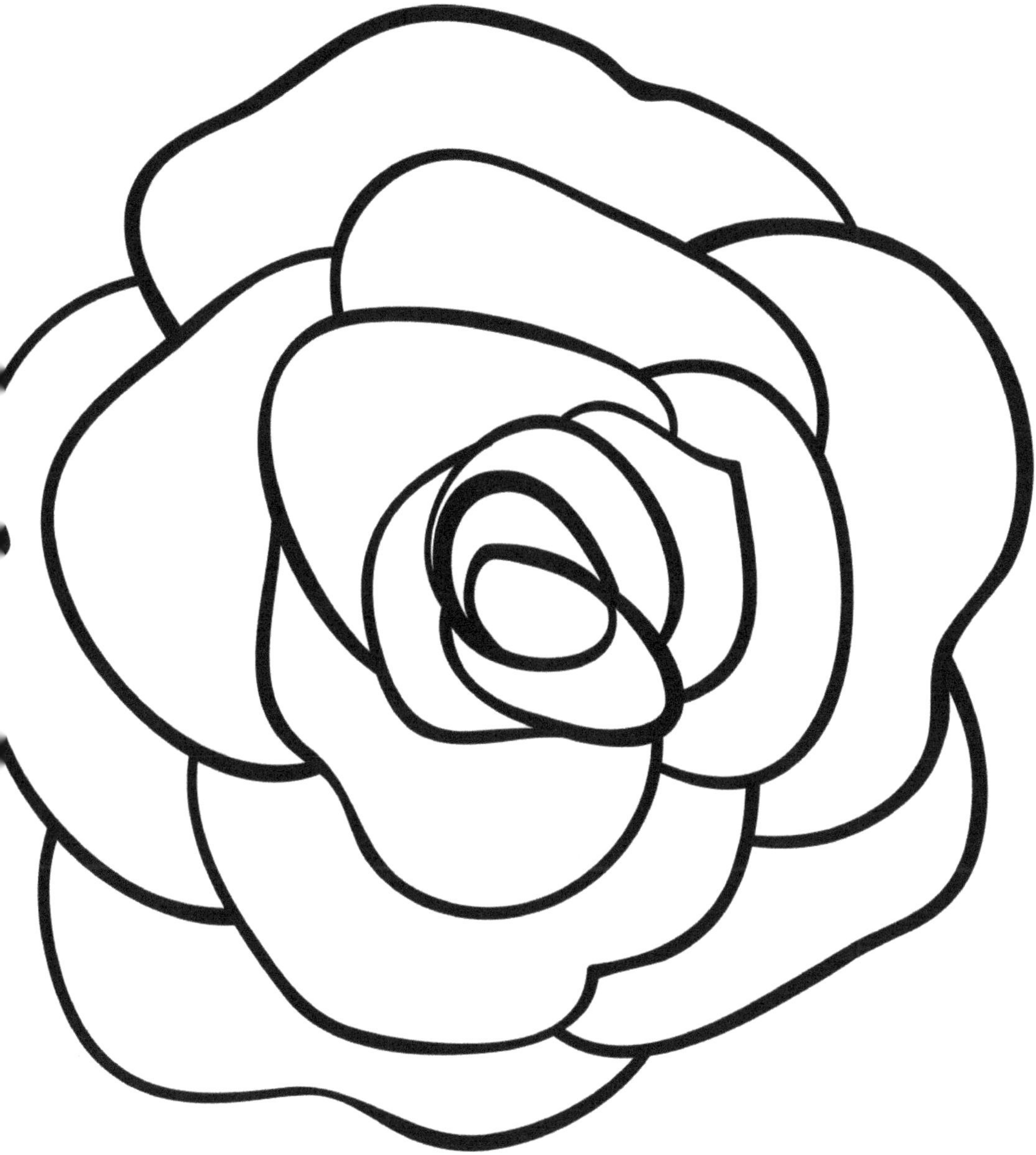

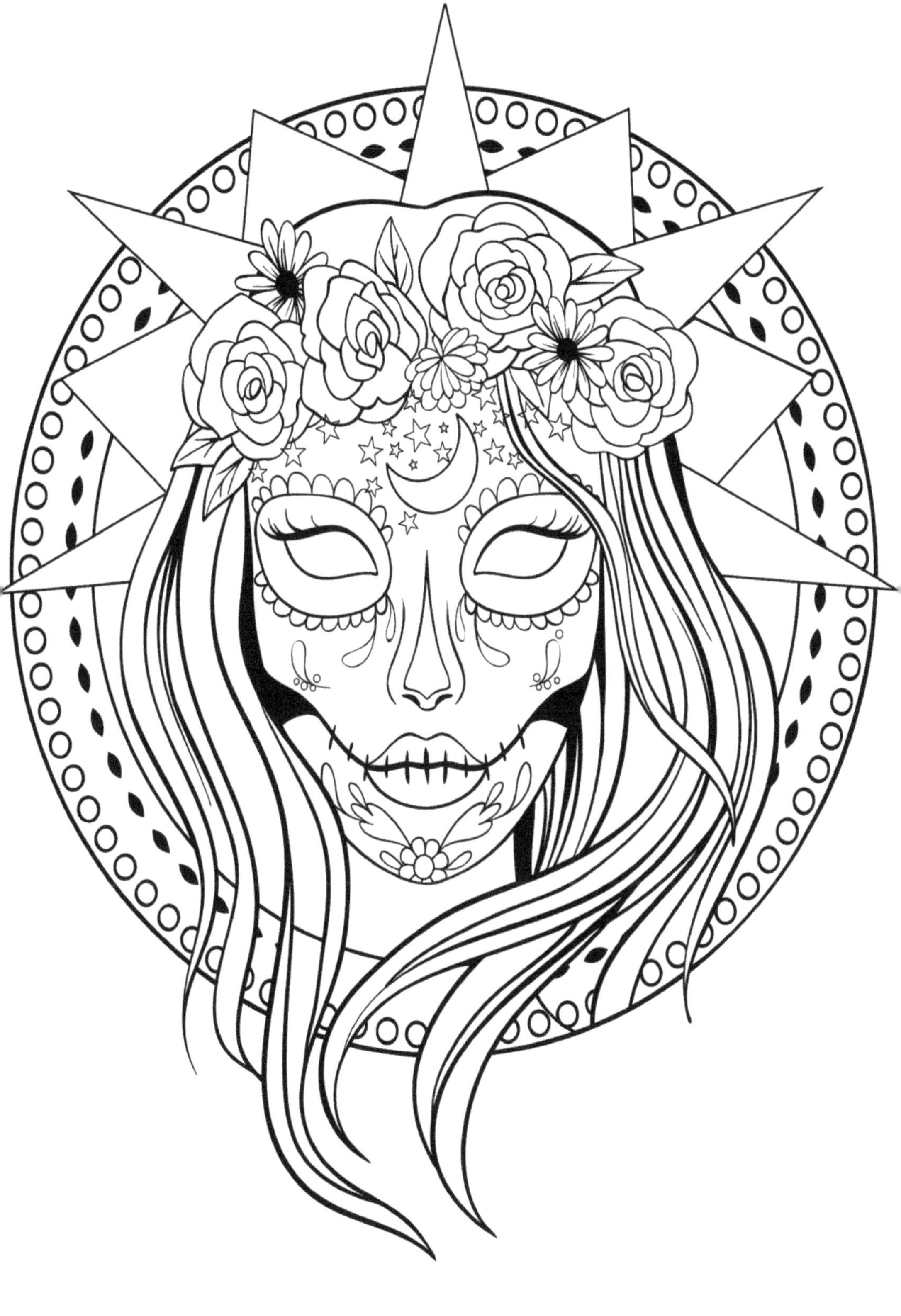

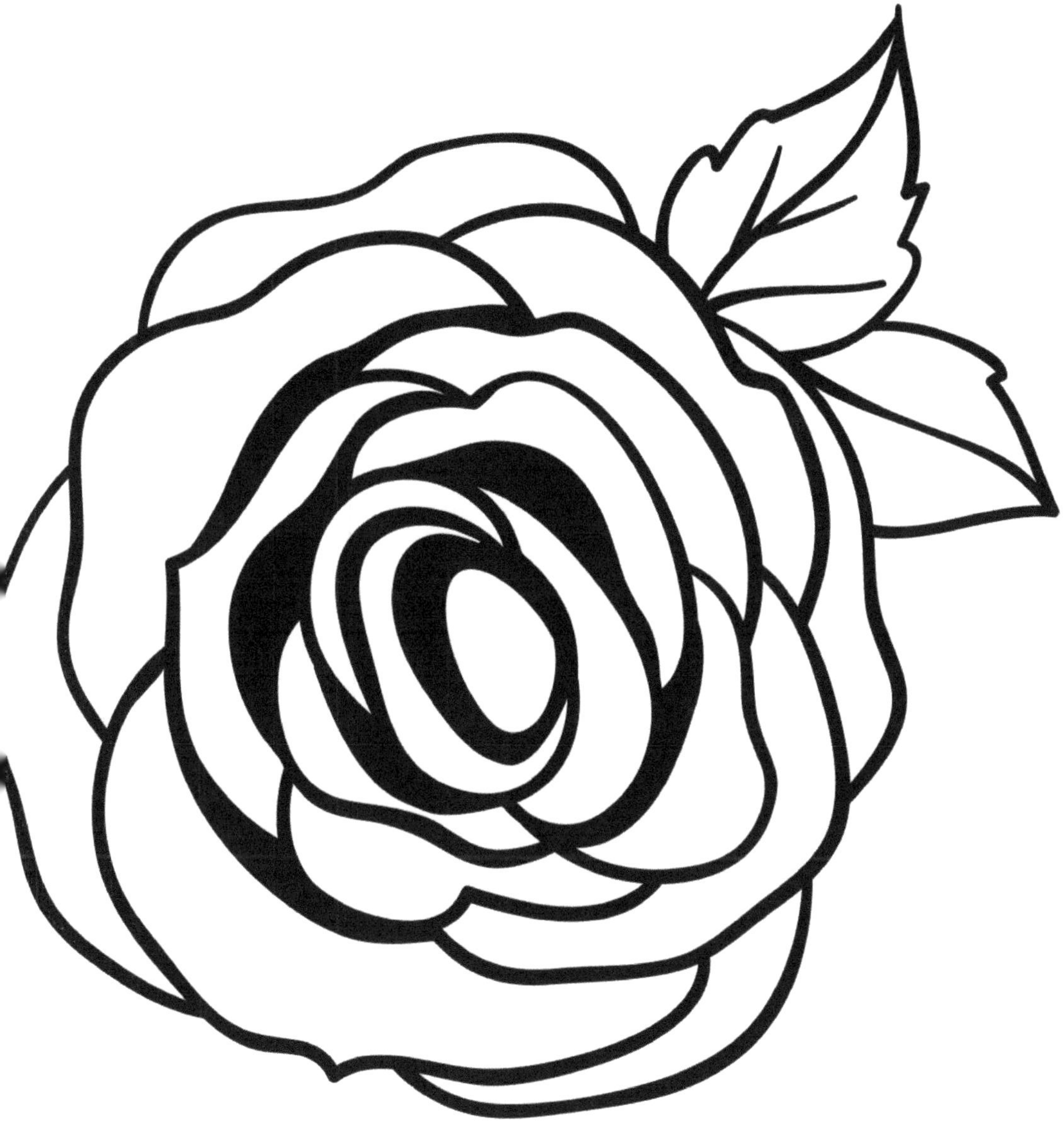

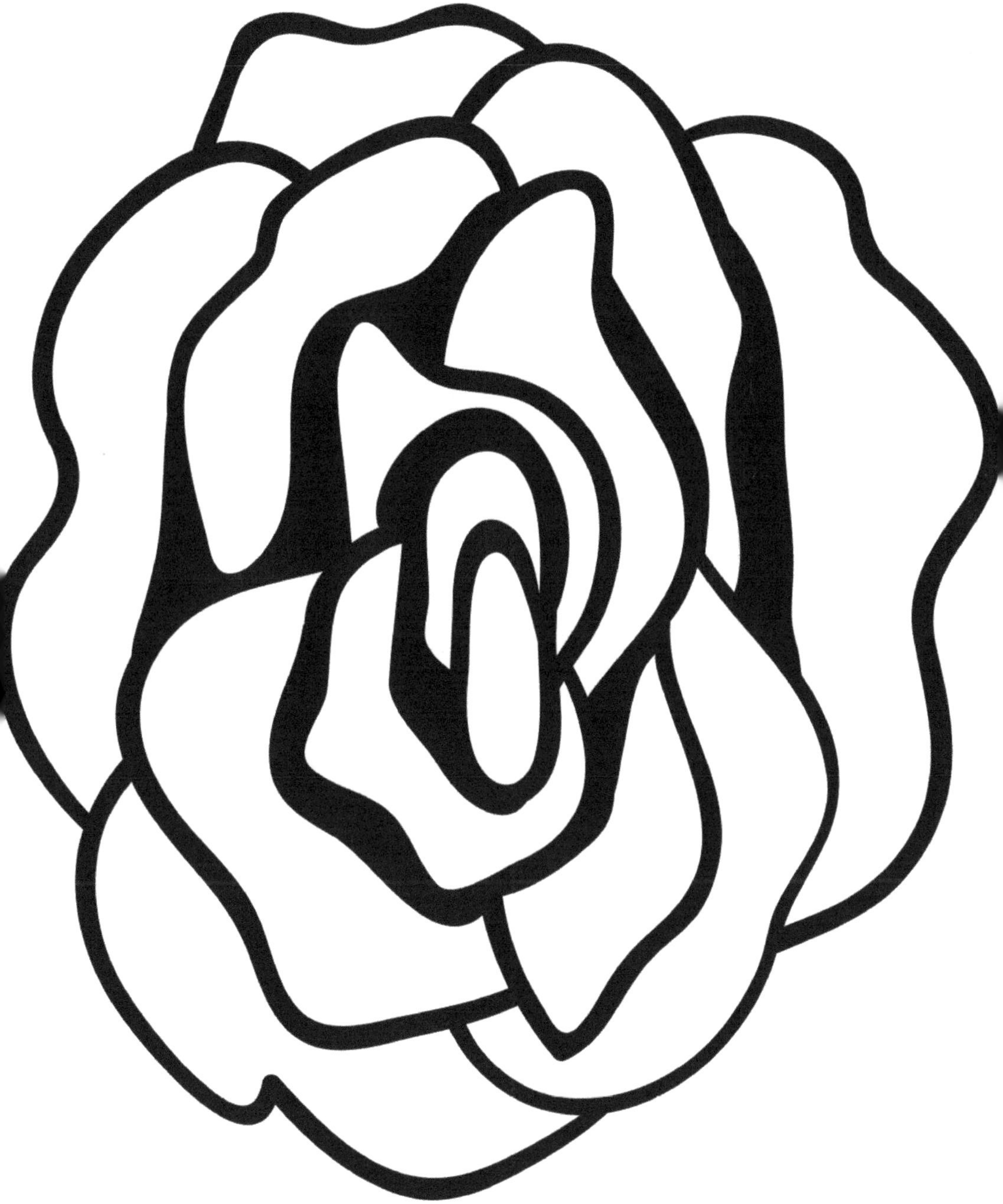

Lightning Source UK Ltd.
Milton Keynes UK
UKHW020805160620
364898UK00003B/173

9 781222 270716